The Complexities of Girlhood

Also by Gracie Drew
Picking Weeds and Calling Them Flowers

The Complexities of Girlhood

Gracie Drew

for the girls who want to be more.

Content Warning

This book contains themes such as sexual abuse, neglect, self-harm, suicidal ideation, obsessive-compulsive thoughts, anxiety, depression, and other potentially triggering material. Please read with care and caution. Thank you.

foreword

i've spent the last six months of my life writing this collection. writing fresh poems about things that still hurt despite not being new wounds. i am known for picking at scabs that don't need to be opened. ones that don't deserve to be remembered. it would be a lie to say it was easy to write this book. it took me so long to find the words. words that weren't repetitive and saying all the same things. essentially, there are only so many ways to say i've been hurt and those things continue to not only hurt, but confuse me. this is not meant to be a complete explanation of everything i've been through, nor should it be used to attempt to understand who i am.

to tell the truth, writing this collection taught me a lot about myself, but despite the many lessons pulled from each poem, i still hate identity and the way it throws me off course. i am not who i was when i started writing these poems and i will never be that girl again. i am so thankful yet so resentful of this truth. i've been force. ive been brave and did things scared. i've written bad poetry that i wasn't proud of and i will continue to do so. im learning that its okay to not be a great big thing. that i am not someone with a huge purpose who is meant to change or save the world. i am meant for such small things and im trying to be proud of that. of the little things i am capable of.

i'm so torn between continuing to share my work with the world and cowering into myself, shutting everything out but my own shadow. but even this i will remain afraid of. what im trying to say is, i hope you like this enough to read it through and understand where i come from when i say girlhood is such a tangle of roots that are meant to be pulled up and re-planted in a different spot from time to time. i've had to accept that i will never be able to stay in the same place. i will never be the woman who settles into a home for the long term with children running around that are identical to my husband. i am all scream and cry. i am a sensitive ball of self-awareness with all the urge in the world to break the cycle. this means things will hurt and they will change, and they will never feel right because they are new to my line of blood. it's all biological is something herapy taught me. you cannot stop the wanting. i cannot stop the missing of my mother and the anger of looking like a spitting image of my father.

for years i spent so much time not understanding what being a woman meant for me specifically. i was always looking for answers on online forums and pathetic google searches late in the night when i couldn't sleep. not understanding why i wasn't doing it the right way. being here and sharing this with you is all about me learning that there is no right way to be or do anything. it all just is what it is and maybe that is an okay thing. maybe we will all be okay no matter the shape our pasts and futures take.

The Complexities of Girlhood

even poets get bored

because there are only so many ways
to write about how the salty air
reminds me of my childhood
and how I miss days with my mother and even
days with my father.
i wish i could go to the beach
and think about other things
that don't sting.
i want my life to stop being this repetitive thing
of self-discovery followed by self-sabotage
that leaves me looking at my own hands
as if i don't know them. as if i don't want to.

damage

being wrapped up in bed
should be simple and even a little
sweet
but there is a twinge of what might be
stuck in my throat
and i didn't mean to be
so many broken things.

gentle

i knew my life needed to change
but i didn't know how to become the person
who could do it.
the girl i was back then,
back in my teenaged bedroom,
sat in candlelight and
wrote about boys i really thought
i'd love forever.

in florida, it storms often and hard
and when it would pour,
i'd sit on my front porch,
the one that wrapped
around the house,
and read.

sometimes now, in the boston thunderstorms,
i miss her and it riddles me with
an aching sensation.
if only i could go back to who i was
and shake some life into her.
make her into something that's kinder to herself.
because she was soft, she was gentle,
but she found love in the sickest places
and in every corner but her own.

gracie (the girl you wanted to be)

but could never get quite right.
so, you pick at her.
dissect her like her skin
would fit you on every side.
it's so easy to be a girl
and never forgive yourself
for it.

to be perfect is to be a woman
who knows how to cry to herself.
you wanted this to be easy.
you want to be able to admit
that you're not what you
always thought you'd be.

but your mother never taught you
self-preservation.
you didn't grow up with
a teethy smile and braids in
your hair.
you grew up with empty
spaces and knowing the sound
of everyone's footsteps.
now you're twenty-something
and trying to remember childhood
and what it means
to have missed out on
the normalcy of girlhood.

It's so easy to be
a girl and never
forgive yourself for it.

in new york

i walk down vast streets
and sip coffee that burns
my tongue but tastes
like heaven.
there are strangers i smile at
and think about long after
they're gone.
i like to people watch
and learn about myself
at train stations and
in the back of the taxi i take
to and from the job i love.
i dance on my tip toes around
my tiny apartment and
it doesn't hurt.
the girl i am is simple
and even a little sweet.
she is who i have always
wanted to be
but have never had
the courage
to introduce myself
to.

i'm not ready for womanhood

without my mother,
i am not ready
for womanhood.
without her to teach me
the act of self-preservation
and caring about
what happens to me,
i don't know that i can
keep growing up.
there is no way to forgive her
for the way i am just
like her.
i am so tired of the space
i miss her in.

what if i'm the only exception to stability

in the fist of august,
i can't breathe.
i need to be brave enough
to face myself in the faint
bathroom light
early in the morning.
i think it doesn't get
better for me.

to be a perfect woman

i am trying to learn how to cry
only when i'm alone.
to be brave and strong and
a perfect woman.
i think about my body.
the twists and curves of
adulthood.
i don't know what i am
but i know that it hurts
when i am face to face with
the girl in the mirror
each morning.
i brush my hair as a way
to take care of myself.
to remind myself that
i am more than just alive.
there is courage and then
there is throwing up
from the realization that
i will always be just a step behind
the woman i wish i was.

this is what your 20s are for

its 8pm and i'm ready for bed. i haven't liked staying up late since i was fourteen. i am not the kind of girl to want to be seen. i live in a silence. in a way that makes you wonder if i exist or if i'm just a figment of your imagination. this isn't all i want to be. there is nothing else.

endings

it felt like i was slowly
losing myself and i didn't know
what to do with the parts of me
that didn't mind the dying.
it was because of love
that i became a victim
in the first place.
it was because i couldn't tell
the difference between
being brave and being kind
that i lost my body.
in each crevice of trying to get better,
i blame myself.
i look at who i am and
see the gaps in her.
i feel bad for her.
but i can't cry over it
anymore.
i can't be surprised
when i've seen the ending
so many times.

the loneliness sets in

how alone i was
made me sick
and there was
no one to blame
but myself.

the loneliness sets in

how alone i was
made me sick
and there was
no one to blame
but myself.

I hope that I will
wake up as someone
who doesn't need to
be needed.

the face of a girl

i have to be happy for myself
and what i'm doing
because there is no one here
to see me
get better.
i have to encourage myself
to live life at least a little bit
longer.
i am on my own
in the big gaps of
my apartment
and it's enough
because it must be.
because at the end
of every long and dreadful
monday,
i curl up into my bed
and hope that tomorrow
i will not notice the silence
as harshly.
i hope that i will wake up
as someone who doesn't need
to be needed.

I beg to recall
like when it
was easier.

what am i going to be?

they say
you'll never be
as young as you are
today
and in a way, or a lot,
i am thankful that time
passes and heals
the many parts of me
that think being loved
will save me.
i hope when i get old,
i remember the ways
i smiled and laughed
the kind of laughs
that hurt.
i beg to recall life when
it was easier.
there are ways around
being alive
and today i will sip tea
and remind myself of
the slowness.
i will stay alive and i will do it
intentionally.

i try to find compassion for her

because i know she's just a woman
with her own line of misery.
i come to understand her
because as i get older,
i realize how hard it is
to want to keep going.
how delicate life and yourself
is.

vanish

sometimes i think about
running away from the life
i have built for myself for
the past twenty-three years.
tearing down my closet and
packing a single bag full of
all of my memories
and abandoning the city
that saved me at one point.
i don't know why i keep
coming back to this part.
maybe it's dissatisfaction,
maybe i'm just not ready
to be happy.
maybe everything
i've ever loved
will leave me
in the end
and i need to be the one
to make a run for it
before i hear the click
of a closing door and
twist of a lock.

stupid woman

sometimes i feel
like a stupid woman
with her heart too open.
i think i need to water down
my emotions and
feel a little less.

the lies we tell girls

that boy in middle school
who makes fun of your teeth
and the color of your hair
is not the love of your life
even if your mother says so.
he is not who you will
come home to when you are
thirty and entering your own
version of motherhood.
right now, this will break your heart.
but it's for the better that you
don't fall into the same habits
she did when she was so young
that she never knew how
to grow out of them.

my body is how i say i'm sorry

i used to surrender my body
to angry men in hopes that
they would spare me for
a little longer if maybe they just
got what they ultimately wanted
from me.
it didn't matter what i felt or
if i was scared.
what was important was that
they were happy.
they were kept at bay
and that mattered more to me
than my own body.

you'll never win the war

i wanted to be the girl
who could do it all.
i wanted to be the girl
who became the woman
who didn't care what people
thought about her
and who knew what she
wanted.
i was hoping that by now
i would know who i am.
that i would be at least neutral
about what i have
managed to become.
but most days i don't feel
strong and i have no idea
what i want.

i am who my mother was at my age

when i think about my mother
and her past,
i think about the days she must've
spent scared and alone.
how she sat on the couch of her house
waiting for my father to come home.
i see too much of myself in her.
this is where the problem starts.

it's never enough

being a girl is
never enough
but it's something you think
will fix you.
it's as if growing up
and taking a certain shape
will make you feel better
about the things you have
loved and lost.

i wanted to feel better about myself so

i took an everything shower and tried shaving my legs using butter-milk soap. i lit a candle that smells like apple fritter and washed my hair with eucalyptus shampoo. in this moment i am the epitome of trying to get better. this is me pulling the icky parts of myself away from each other and washing them down the sink drain. i don't want to stay broken forever. i want to feel differently about myself and the things that make up everything i've been for the past twenty-three years. i dim the lights in my apartment and i take up space in every empty gap that i usually wish was filled with something else. some-thing other than me. i even eat a slice of vanilla cake and play jazz that makes me think of a city that i've never been to. things feel simple because they are. i am less sensitive and more under control of my emotions. i am who i am and i like what that means. i am who i am and it has nothing to do do with where i came from. i wanted to feel better about myself so i did.

I don't know
how to settle
in my body
anymore.

i can't forgive myself for who i have loved and been

every sunday morning,
i wake up with a sore throat
and dry, itchy eyes.
there is a vast past behind me.
one i can't forget or forgive.
i've spent so much time breaking
and dying and dealing with
the aftermath of my emotions
that i don't know how to
settle in my body anymore.
i am always running from something
and it always looks like myself.

the complexities of girlhood

at sixteen,
i thought i was done
growing.
that i had done all the learning
there is to do.
but at almost twenty-three
i am still figuring myself out.
trying to piece together
the complexities of girlhood
and wanting to know more
about myself
just as much as i want to
avoid my reflection for the rest
of my life.
i don't know how to become
fond of myself.
i just know it takes a long time
to accept what you cannot change.

is there anything else?

there must be a silver lining
somewhere in the middle
of growing up
a girl.
there has to be more than just
the surviving and then
the remembering that comes
after.

I am a ball of
Fragility.
something you walk
away from.

the girl that i am

i am never where i want to be
in my sensitivities.
there are so many parts of me
that i can't get ahold of.
they run free and i wish i could
let myself be.
i am a ball of fragility.
something you walk away from
because you are tired of
how much i cry
and how much i beg.

if i was prettier

maybe i think about
my side profile more than
i should
but i grew up being taught
that my body is where it all
starts and ends.
that how i look matters more
than keeping myself alive.

it's easy to lie to yourself

i remember thinking the city
would save me.
that broad skylines could
pick me up and make me
fall in love with the act of breathing.
but the truth is,
i was just desperate
and needy.
i used to lay in a gloomy
living room, on a pull-out sofa
and fall with my own breath.
things felt slower.
safer.
even if they weren't.

what does it mean to be a girl

i am always avoiding
my own hands.
always looking the
other way
when i catch a glimpse of
the way i cut my hair
and forgot who i am
for all those years.
i am still coming back
to myself
and in many ways
i don't want to.

I am still
unlearning her
childhood. Still
prying it from
my own.

it reminds me of my mother to call myself a girl

i think my hair being long makes me worthy of being loved / i miss my mother brushing it and letting me cut my bangs even though i would always regret it / she taught me a lot about impulses and falling apart / i remember crying when the knots got so big that we had to trim them out / or that time she put my hair up in a bun for the first time and i thought it made me the most beautiful thing / i felt so grown up / i felt like a woman so young / she made me think life was both worth it and not / i am still unlearning her childhood / still prying it from my own.

i'm just a girl

i know it's repetitive to say
i wish my teeth were different
and that my freckles were
a little less prominent
but what is there if not self-loathing?
what do i do with the parts of my body
that i can't fathom will be loved?
how do i come back from
destroying myself
so many times?
do i expect someone to love me
when i can't like myself?
there are so many ways to be a girl
and none of them fit.
there are so many ways to fall apart
and not enough to put myself
back together.

growing up a girl

i am unlearning the hard edges
and broken pieces
of growing up a girl.
it's hard to stomach
the passing days
during the warmer months
of the year
when it reminds me of
summers with my father
and late nights catching
fireflies.
i can't say it was all bad.
but it could've been easier.
it could've been softer.
i could've been.

I will never be able to escape where I come from.

i am all my mother

there is no place like
that pit in my stomach
that reminds me
that i will always be
at least a little bit like
my mother on the inside.
despite my red hair
and bright freckles
that are reminiscent
of my father,
i am all my mother.
it's in the way that i cry
when i'm angry
and how ashamed i get
when it sets in that
i will never be able to escape
where i come from.

i hate the color pink

i grew up wanting
to be like the other girls.
the ones who chewed on
bubblegum until their jaws
were sore and
had hair so long that they
spent most of their time bragging
about how long it took them
to grow it out.
being a girl came so naturally to them.
it was like they were doing it right
and i was doing it wrong.
i started to hate the way
my hair parted on my head
and the clothes my mom
would buy me.
i stopped going to school
and started fearing my own
body.
all i wanted was to be liked
and i couldn't give it to myself.
i didn't want to.
i wanted to be the girl who
could spin on her toes and
feel everything but not say
a word about it.

i am trying

to be a better girl.
a more put together girl.
one that's missed the second
she leaves the room.
but i have never been these things.
i have never had the stomach
to ask myself how to get better.
i am so far from the finish line.
i don't know how i will die
but i can say that i wish i did.

wanted

i've spent most of my time
trying to be loved
and wanting to be needed.
to be wanted.

forgiveness

i grew up so mighty.
i was stubborn and i knew how
to yell at my father and talk back
to my mother.
some days, as a twenty-three
year old,
i hope my mother can forgive me
for the ways i slammed my
bedroom door
after a stupid fight and let go
of her hug before
she was ready
to let go of me.

chilly

it is tuesday and
i am falling witness
to my own suffering.
i want to be able to
take care of myself.
to wrap my arms around
my own existence and
be okay with the fact
i am taking up space.
i didn't mean to be so loud
or to want as much as i do
but it's so cold out
and it makes me miss
the version of myself
i could've been if i grew up
in a softer place.

secrets intact

i learned a lot about
keeping my mouth shut
as a girl.
i think my mother knew a lot
about it too.
in these ways
i can't blame her.
she was only teaching me
what she knew.
all she knew.

maybe I don't deserve
the things I want

i want to be a pretty girl

my skin is getting so dry
from the winter coming along
and i am so scared of
my own body.
the way i enter a rocm
without turning heads
and how i laugh while
hiding my teeth
is enough to make me feel
like maybe i don't deserve
the things i want.

you don't know what you have til' it's gone

in my office, at my big age,
i sit with my hair in a sad excuse
of a pony tail
and write poems about growing up
and wishing i had a home to go back to.
with a candle lit, and the lighting just right,
maybe this is all i've ever wanted
without realizing it.

you don't know what you have til' it's gone

in my office, at my big age,
i sit with my hair in a sad excuse
of a pony tail
and write poems about growing up

the girl i was will die with me

i had to grow up eventually.
i had to not only let go
of the girl i was
but i had to twist the knife.
it was only right
to make myself suffer.
it was easier to kill myself
than to watch as my
parents did it for me.

it's that time of year

i've been abandoning myself
for as long as i can remember.
during the colder months,
i wrap myself in a blanket
and miss the girl
i could've been.
the one i almost was.
who i would've been if
only i was stronger.

i cry in my bed and ask for my mother

if i could only tell you one thing about girlhood,
it would be that i have spent most of it
dissecting my mother and missing her.

insatiable

i am stuck in a loop of desire.
i want what i can't have.

I am all rage
and no girl

gone girl monologue

i can be bloody.
i can be all teeth and back talk.
i am all rage and no girl.

i'm being the cool girl

in this version of the story
i am not the me i've been.
i am not messy-headed and
scared of being in my apartment alone.
my teeth are less crooked
and my freckles don't remind me
of my father.
in an ideal world, i am a little taller
and a little less emotional.
i am not driven by my fears and
i can love without becoming a victim
to a betrayal that isn't there.
i am casual and admirable.
i am the woman that the little girl
sees on the street and can't wait to be

one day.

love of your life

i was raised by a mother who thought
being bullied meant you were being loved.

the version of myself where no one is watching

here
i drink iced coffee
topped with cold foam
without gagging at the taste.
here
i walk down the street
all on my own
and keep my head high.
here
my hair is just past my chin
and doesn't get darker
in the winter.
here
i never worry about
being enough.

on being sad all the time

i grew up with a crooked mother and an empty father. i watched her become a fire in front of my very eyes and i watched him as he stopped loving me. it's like i saw it slip from his face one random day and i didn't know how to be the girl who could win people over. who could make people love her. back to my mother and her flame. back to my childhood, where i relive the fear all over again. you never learn how to let go of a lack of love. i think i knew she didn't like me when i was around fourteen. and with my father, it was always obvious that he hated me. that he hated women and was determined to let me know it.

I didn't know how
to be the girl
who could win people
over

red lipstick

i think i'd be prettier
and worth loving a little more
if i did my makeup more often
and let my hair grow long again.
because here at midnight,
i am in a state of hating my body.
of being scared of not being
a girl worth seeing.

the way i hate myself reminds me of little me

and i think she'd be disappointed.
when i think about this,
i start to cry harder.
i start to groan with
each tear i shed.
i can feel my heart breaking
over everything
we should've been
if only i had a little bit
more fight left in me.

i feel like such a girl right now

after a fresh shower,
i get into clothes that i never
could've worn when i was
a teenager
and spray too much perfume.
my top is off the shoulder and
a little cropped.
i feel like such a girl right now.
this is what i've always wanted;
to be a woman and love myself
despite it.

to be a woman
  and love myself
despite it

detransition, i guess

my shoulders feel
too broad
and my voice feels too
harsh
and i never really got over
the way i lost myself
all those years.

i have to be a big girl

i keep telling myself
that i need to be brave.
that i need to learn how to cry
on my own and wipe my own
tears when a boy breaks my heart.
i wrap my arms around myself
and try to make that enough.

competing

if my mother taught me anything
it was that there was no such thing
as a girls girl.

cupping my hands to
a curtain-less window
and watching all
     the hurt

the end of the world

when i feel alone,
i read my old journal entries
and ache for myself.
i imagine myself as an outsider,
cupping my hands to a curtain-less
window and watching all the hurt
that goes on inside.
there are puddles of tears flooding
an empty living room and boats
full of confusion and anger treading
the waters.
i watch her be lonely in the midst of
what feels like the end of the world.

i am so in love with being a victim

that i don't let myself feel better.
i don't sit in a beautiful home
surrounded by people who love me
and feel it.
i am too occupied with the what ifs
and full of what has already happened.

friday

throwing tennis balls in the backyard
for my dog to flail herself at
and sleeping in late because the night before
was a hard one.
as i start to write,
i become less heavy.
i am less fear and more girl.
i worry it won't always feel this way
and i'm always being reminded that
it isn't normal to be happy all the time
but for right now,
i make it enough
to know that i can be okay sometimes.
in the gaps of my anxiety lives
someone who wants to live so much longer
than she is meant to.

white tile shower walls

i find myself on the shower floor
again.
i am trying to piece together
my day and maybe even myself.
was i happy?
was my anxiety a little too
noticeable at the kitchen counter?
did i need to change anything
about myself to make sure
the love stays?

did I need to change anything about myself to make sure the love stays?

it's only me

i'm trying to learn how to be happy
when i am the only one there
to see it.
sometimes i feel like i need to prove
that i exist.
that i am not just some ghost
hunched over a burnt coffee,
carrying anger that should've
dissipated by now.

harsh truths

i didn't know who i was
for the longest time.
i thought i was nothing
and then i thought i was too much
and i believed every man who
told me so.

i didn't know who i was
for the longest time.
i thought i was nothing

shampoo and conditioner combo

i can sing my heart out
and dance until the bottoms
of my feet are worn out
and still want to keep going.
how beautiful is it to want to live
after knowing the beauty of death?

I cry too much
and too hard

apologies

all i could get out
were apologies and
it was never enough
to make up for the way
i cry too much
and too hard
and over the little things
or even things that
aren't there
to begin with.

a casual girl

i didn't know what to say.
i just knew i wasn't everything
everyone wanted me to be.
a stable girl.
a cool girl.
a casual girl.
in some ways, i let myself down.

high maintenance

growing up a little girl, i was told i was high maintenance. i was called bossy and annoying and ugly. each of them stung in different ways. i couldn't protect myself without being told safety wasn't an option. i swore the boys who picked on me the most loved me the biggest and that wasn't even my first mistake. the first was believing my father wanted to see me for who i was; a smaller version of him, one that was deserving of at least a little love.

it's that kind of night again

if i were to ask anything
i think it would be
why do i find myself needing
to crawl onto the bathroom floor
to cry more than
i feel deserving to cry
in a lovers arms.

it's that kind of night again

if i were to ask anything
i think it would be
why do i find myself needing

i used to want my mom
to scoop me up and
tell me being sensitive
was a good thing

the urge to hide in the shower is stronger than the urge to call my mother

i used to want my mom
to scoop me up
and tell me being sensitive was
a good thing.
that it made me brave
and beautiful.
instead i am so old
and so small
all at once.

a sense of belonging

i could be so many things
and yet none of them would be
enough to please
the critic in me
that sounds a lot like
the boys in my middle school
telling me that i would never be
the girl they found pretty enough
to want to call their own.
now that i'm older
i try to pinpoint why it was so
important to me
that i was anyone's other than
my own.

I am some of
my mother's
sadness

leaving and growing up

for the longest time,
i thought it was my fault
to want to leave home.
i thought trying to find
escape routes
made me evil.
like i wasn't grateful enough.
but the truth has always been
that i am some of my mother's sadness
and all of my father's abandonment.

*i wanted more and it ended up not being all i thought it
would be*

it's never been easy
to remember where
i come from.
i feel i have been made
too soft and too often
devastated by my own desire
to ever achieve anything
tangible.
it is as though nothing important to me
really matters in the big world
around me.
it's almost as if i am trying so hard to become
something i never was going to have
the possibility of understanding.

I can't tell what is me
and what is wound

what is me

i am so familiar with
sickness.
i was too young
to remember my grandmother
after i lost her
but i'd like to think
she watches over me
and believes me when i say
i have been hurt so deep
that i can't tell what is me
and what is wound.

something about tears

i hate the days
where i feel like i can't breathe
and like if i start crying
i would never stop.
i was hoping i'd be
more gentle by now.
but i am a scream and cry
kind of a girl.
a beg you to love me and stay
kind of girl.

I am a scream and
cry kind of girl.

holidays

at this time
each year
i feel so much less
than whole.
i feel as though
my fragments have
divided into their own
pile of shards.

hoax

i thought i could love you into loving me.

intensity

it's been easy to
love the things i love
but it doesn't come
without consequence.
sometimes i am the girl
throwing up from her sadness
and other times i am vibrating
and buzzing with a will to live
so strong that it might save you too.

growing up has to get easier (i hope)

i wanted to understand more by now. i was hoping that by now, i would be someone so brave and strong that it didn't matter how scary something was. that i could face where i come from without getting sick to my stomach with sadness. i never prepared myself for my mother still being a little evil and my brothers being a thing of the past. sometimes when i am nothing, i think about the times we spent laughing and wandering the neighborhood a little too late at night. admiring the christmas lights in the winter and talking about how one day we will be better. less sick.

the bathroom in atlanta is a little emptier

i find myself on the bathroom floor again.
trying to hold back all of my tears
in the dark and on the cold tile.
i am so scared of being scared.
of never getting over this.
all of it.

the bathroom in atlanta is a little emptier

i find myself on the bathroom floor again.
trying to hold back all of my tears
in the dark and on the cold tile.
i am so scared of being scared.

i hope I forget
all the time I spent
worrying over things
that were never going
to really kill me

death bed

i hope i die
with no regrets.
at least not so many
that i am scared of taking
my last breath.
i hope i forget
all the time i spent
worrying over things that
were never going to really
kill me.

changing

so, i am trying to be the kind of woman who makes friends easily
and doesn't mind her own loud laugh. i hope to one day stop winc-
ing at my own softness. i walk around department stores shopping
for clothes i never thought i'd feel safe enough to wear and it's true
that i'm still scared but i'm less child now. i am taller and braver. it
has become more natural for me to live for myself.

i don't want to hurt the ones who love me

there are a lot of days
where i am so much sickness
that i can't fathom a moment
of freedom.
my chest will slam up and down
and i will be forced to keep going.
i will still find a way to resent those who

love me.

the city of boston

i have to realize at some point
that it is all about what i want
and what i choose to do.
i've learned that they aren't
the same thing.
the time i have spent being scared
feels so stupid in the moments where
the view is big and beautiful.

fake it til' you make it

sometimes i go into the bathroom
just to stare myself in the face
and try to remind myself that
i'm real.
it's so hard to believe that
i made it out alive.
even though sometimes i will tell you
that there was nothing to survive.
that my mother was gentle and my father
was there, arms wide open.
this is how i trick myself.
i've realized that i can't remember and live
at the same time.

I made it
out alive.

we are leaving to go home today

and i'd be happy if
this drive never ended
and i never had to make up
my mind.

homesick, maybe

i am always running
to new places
and hoping they will
bring me ease.
i'm never happy
with where i am.

being brave is another story

what if i'm always
wanting more
or something other than
what i have in front of me.
i don't want to spend my life waiting
yet here i am
bundled up in the fact that i will die
with many regrets and
so many things unsaid.

l dont want
to spend my
life waiting

i have to understand that i'm safe now

i wanted to be every other girl. i thought it would make me import-
ant, special and beautiful to be someone who wasn't me. someone
who didn't cry this much. someone who knew what they wanted and
went for it when they finally saw it. instead, i'm a coward. instead,
i'm a girl who doesn't fit into this idea of womanhood. i am far from
perfect and far from what a lover wants. i am both too much and too
little to be tangible at the same time. how does anyone love someone
so confusing? someone so full of their own victimization that they
don't realize they're safe now, and have been for a while?

where it all starts

most of my poetry starts in the notes app on my phone, written from the shower, with tears welling in my eyes. it's a lot of trying not to cry. of trying to ignore the fact that i'm not as happy as i should be.

i want to see my mother's childhood

i wish i could cup my mother's childhood
in my hands
and watch where it all
swerved off path.
to see the moment she began to feel
smaller than she was.

i want to see my mother's childhood

i wish i could cup my mother's childhood
in my hands
and watch where it all

it snowed today

and i feel better than i did yesterday.
it's the first snow of the year
and i spent it holed up
in my apartment alone.
there has been no one to see me
keep myself alive and so
the only one who can be
proud of me
is me.

i'm still not all i thought i was

i wanted to be loved
for my quirks
and the things i have always believed
made me something that needed to be fixed.
instead, i am in a dimly lit room
waiting for myself to come home.

I am in a dimly
lit room waiting
for myself to
come home.

is all that's left the poetry?

there needs to be a greater reason
that i feel this way.
a way to make all of these grand learning curves
into something worth more than me.
because the pain has always been so much bigger
than my body and there are only so many ways
i can morph into something stronger.

tears

i cried tonight
and it did not
bring back my mother
or undo my father.

tears

i cried tonight
and it did not
bring back my mother
or undo my father.

lying to girls

how easy was it for you to tell me you love me and that you'd never leave me knowing that one day, very soon, you'd be gone for good?

the skeleton in the closet was always just me

i wonder what is wrong with me
when i sit criss-cross on my living room floor
doing nothing but watching myself crawl
out of my own skin and abandon the leftovers.

watching myself
crawl out of
my own skin
and abandon the
leftovers.

forgive me

when i am ugly crying
and cannot face myself in the dim-lit
mirror,
will you wish you had left
before you were more used to my screeching
sobs and heavy eyes?
will i spend my life being your biggest regret?

the 2024 year is coming to an end

and i'm not as relieved as i thought i would be at the end of a december and the roaring beginning of a january. to no one's surprise, it is just me and my mind at it again. a little self-deprecating, a lot shameful. i am not much to look at, but i hope to be. i spent a lot of time this year doodling in journals and wishing my writing reflected what i felt better. that it would stop being so repetitive and more worth reading, or writing in the first place. my poetry is where i go to forgive myself. it's where i live on the days i cannot stomach the outside world, or even just outside the covers on my never-made bed that i share with a lover i've known for longer than i can remember. my point being, that every year comes and goes and i find myself wishing something would plant itself in my life and stay. not necessarily love me, but see me. to look at me and remind me that despite the fact that everything comes to an end, i still matter.

it took me months

i am still the girl in the back of a chatty classroom.
the one who does not speak unless spoken to.
mostly because she is scared of the perception
that comes with opening your mouth as a girl.

teenage dream

i was supposed to be more grown up
by now.
to be able to hold my own hair back
when i am hung over a toilet and sick from the memories.
i didn't want to be alive, i just wanted
to be different.
i wanted to be someone who
can see more of their childhood
and stomach it.
i thought getting older meant
my body would stop recalling things.
but i've carried it all with me
up until this point and there is nowhere to put the tragedies and
butterfly clips
that i use to hold up my stringy still-growing-it-out hair.
so i bury it deeper into my form.
i let it rot me from the inside out.
i was never going to be who i thought
i'd be by now.

wasn't this supposed to be my year?

please don't forget me
when i am nothing more than a mere
recollection of the things that have
happened to me.

when I am nothing
more than a mere
recollection of the
things that have
happened to me.

christmas day or something like it

i am not sad or angry or anything
other than at peace with the fact
i will never speak to my mother or
see my brothers again.
this time of year, the time of year
where it snows and the cold wind
is more brutal than anything,
is usually so hard. it is usually so heavy
that i don't know how i will carry myself
from room to room.
but today i sit on the floor and make
my own memories and traditions.
i learn that not everything will stay
and that i have to be okay with
letting go.

best day

i remember enough
about being a child
to feel a sense of grief
when i recall how far gone
it is.
almost over night
i grew up and got bigger.
i stopped being daddy's little girl
and eventually i was going to turn
into my mother.
it was only a matter of time
before i realized nothing
ever stays the same.

teenaged twenty somethings

what is it
about growing up
that stings
like chlorine breaking through
your tightly shut eyelids
under the pool water
in your fathers backyard?
how do i skip to the part
where i know how to be alive
without hoping it ends soon?
where do i have to go
in order to find the part of me
that swore this would never

happen to her?

genetics and other tragedies

it's woven in fate that i would never get better. it's not enough to want. to have desires is to admit defeat. i feel sick as i turn over in my bed and wish to be loved. it's almost pathetic how much i wish things could have been different. not really better, but just different. maybe i would be less scared. less small and forgetful. i hate the part of my life where i hope. i am always trying to think of other things. i fall into my mothers old habits and to some extent i hate myself for it. but it was inevitable to end up like someone so fragile. i was never going to be strong.

i write poetry in my bed hoping things will change

because i hate taking my medication
and i don't want to be someone
who needs anything or anyone.
i want to be as tall as my body.
but i am such a kid who just wants
to live to see the end of the story.

maybe i never was me

i grew up because i had to / it didn't come naturally / it was forced /
i was never brave / maybe i never was me to begin with / softness is
such a weakness / i see myself as so small / yet i can never disappear
enough.

I was never brave.

unlearning

i wanted to be loved.
to be wanted.
but i realized
that i didn't know
how to be.

in the middle of the night

i'm trying to find ways
to break apart
on my own.
at some point
i need to be brave enough
to bear the feeling of not knowing
when things will feel okay again.

when the world is asleep

i am so tired
yet i cannot get
my heavy eyes
to close long enough
to drift off.
i am so full of something
that wants to live.
something that never finds me
at the right times.
it is only ever when
i need to rest
that i want to get up
and move the furniture around
in attempt to create a sense
of newness.
it is only when i imagine my poetry
written by someone else
that i love it.
why must i turn off the lights
and get under the covers
when there is so much to do
now that no one can see me
do it?

if i wasn't a daughter

i think i'd be able to say
i love you
while looking a lover
in the eye.
i'd be less palpable and more
stubborn.
or maybe just less of a
people pleaser
who is scared of the possibility
of being less than great.
there would be no doubt
that i mattered.
i wouldn't know what to do
with all the free space
i'd have
if i wasn't consumed by
my mother's wounds
and a lonely self hatred.
i'd know how to end
my poems on a high note.
the way i feel would match
what is in front of me.
there would be so much
life ahead of me.
one that is not full of
a sense of impending doom.
i don't know that i'd be better.
i can't say for certain that
i would've turned out healthier.
but it would've been different.
please let it have been different.

the girl i carry inside me

i can only hope
she is proud of how
my skin stretched
and bones grew.
over time
you learn that even though
you thought you had died
back in your childhood bedroom,
you never stopped having a desire
to live.
one so deep down
that on most days
you don't notice it.
even on the ones
you need it the most.

sleeping would mean i feel safe enough in my body to love it

i can't express what
i'm haunted by.
i won't tell you that
i've never wanted to die
but there is a film of hope
that falls over everything

maybe there is
a slight beauty
en sameness.

adjusting

the things that mattered
back when i was thirteen
still do
at my big age.
the way i feel pretty
when i pull my hair up
and out of my face
and how i never really stopped
thinking true love is not only real
but possible for me.
maybe there is a slight beauty
in sameness.
the familiarity keeps me
from feeling like i'm not
good enough to stay for.

the ending to a first love

like a movie i go to
whenever i am sad and
in need of saving, i think
of you.
i find myself relying on the memory
of you to keep me believing that
new things are worth doing.
the reality of loving you
when i was just a girl
wasn't worth the complications
of lingering that i find a decade later.
i don't want to be the girl
with her first love's belongings tucked
into a box
long after they've gone.

sometimes i am less than love and more than a great tragedy

it is the most obvious on days where i don't sleep well or long enough. and on nights where the sun sets so early that i swear i must've missed something. i throw up when i am sad and i wear my mother's abandonment on my face. i am so open with my suffering that somewhere down the line, i started to think it was all i had.

poetry is how i say i'm sorry

if i could apologize to anyone
maybe it would first be
my grandmother and then maybe
myself.

i never learned
how to look someone in the eyes
when admitting i'm wrong.

so, i take my time
jotting down subtle rhymes
and dog earing the pages.
leaving nothing behind but
tear stains and regret.

you can close a journal
but you cannot temporarily end a life.
specifically your own.
no matter how much you think about it.

why i stay alive

i washed my hair today
so now i feel more human.
more loveable and less shameful.
i feel clean in a way
i've been trying to achieve
for years.
nothing ever really works
but if i can count on anything,
it is the way i feel after a shower.
one where i think up poems
and reminisce without the weight
of fear.
there are reasons we live and there
are reasons we stay alive.

i told my therapist i'm doing better

and maybe that wasn't true.
maybe i'm not entirely sure
what it means to be level headed
and stable.
all i know is
i feel weak when i cry
and ugly when i beg.

four feet nothing

every part of me didn't think
i'd make it this far.
that we would live to see the day
things felt easy. fickle. gentle.
and when there are days
that are so far from what
i want for myself,
i try to remember the girl
in me.
the little one who was 4'11
until she was 14
and still hasn't fully grown up.

i hope you remember to be happy

even when there is not much left
to life
but the slowness of the cold months
coming to an end
and rainy days in the spring
that remind you what it means
to keep going.
i hope you remember to
enjoy things as they come
and not only after they have left
for good.
that you can recall your childhood
and feel your face soften instead of
harden in between every summer memory.

pretty

i never knew how
to feel good enough.
starting so young,
i learned how to hurt myself
without wincing at the blood.
i was a little girl trapped
in the lingering body of something
that's been dead for so long
that it can't remember its own

name.

things i inherited from my dad

his heavy fists full of shame.
the freckles on my shoulders.
a body so hollow that my blood echoes.
blazing orange hair that reminds me of my grandmother.

over him

it feels like it's my right
to be sad
and to spend the rest of my life
wishing things were different for
us.

When things were full to the brim with normalcy and overall goodness.

*tip toeing the borderline of ending up like my mother or my
father*

i inherited my fathers freckles
and my mothers inability to know
when it's time to walk away.
i will endure the end of the world
and wake up tomorrow
convinced there is still some
life left.
it's so hard to think about
what they're up to now—if they think
of me.
if they try to remember the sound
of my laugh when things
were full to the brim with
normalcy and overall goodness.
the sensation of hunger is nothing
compared to the gaps in my childhood.
the emptiness i feel when i picture
my mothers old and rickety bed
back in our run-down florida home.
i get a lot from my parents
but not anything i am thankful for.
i try to peel my fathers absence
from my skin.
from the places i have learned
how to hurt myself just right.
i wish the memory of my mother away and
beg her to change all in one
big breath.
there is growing into yourself
and growing out of it
and i worry that no matter
my next move, no matter where
i find myself on a saturday afternoon,
i will always be nothing more than
the devastation they left for me.

mother

if i could ask my mother anything
it would be about things getting better.
if they ever do.
if she ever found herself sitting on the floor
of her first apartment
crying over the possibility of never becoming
anything more than a woman with bite as a father
and silence as a mother.
i wonder this because i am twenty-three
and doing just that.
i don't fall to the floor, i crumble.
and i wrap my knuckles around the idea that
my mother maybe would've had a better chance
if she never had me. if she never became
a mother in the first place.
maybe she would've chosen to get better.
maybe she would've chosen herself.
maybe she would've gotten the life she wanted.

we never kissed

i am the girl in new york who still
loves you.
the one who is pathetic and
doesn't know any better.
i fall for the boys who bare their teeth.
i am only doing what my mother
taught me.
it's so easy to fall in love and so hard
to forget about it.
even when your skin breaks and
you're left with a scar shaped like
your hometown.
the small blip on the map that still
reminds you of your first love.
the damage is done but is it over?

sessions with my therapist

what does crazy mean to you?
the question sits on my chest
and the answer lingers in my throat.
i just don't want to be like my mother.
i say this because i grew up
watching her slowly fall out of love
with herself and her life.
it made her angry and absent
and i can't recall the hurt of it all
without feeling somewhat apologetic
towards her.
it's not your fault.
she tells me this and i don't
believe it.
i was born and i grew up and
in some sick way i never forgave myself
for that part.
for my autonomy and urges to leave
home and never look back.

worrying the
love will
never come,

so close yet so far

i think part of being a girl
is worrying the love
will never come.
that i will always cover my face
with the palms of my hands
and say sorry for wanting.
apologizing for the depth
of my desire.

hair cuts

there is no poetry to write
or way to let myself down easy.
i am devastation coated
in a girl-like film.
i cut my hair because i thought
i would feel better after the fact.
but i left the salon heavier than
i went in and it's true that i
looked different
but i was still carrying
the metaphorical loss
of my mother behind my ears
and my fathers gaze on my shoulders
and i went home to cry
like i've never cried before.

genetics

it is almost 11pm and
i need to be brave and recover
from myself.
from the things i have taught myself
over the years of reliving
my own damned childhood.
my own self hatred shown to me
by my father.

better girl

i try to move on and accept
the things i cannot change.
the ones about us.
the ones about you.
there are only so many parts
of the story that i can keep
to myself.
if i was a better girl
i'd be better at keeping
my mouth shut.

If I was a better girl
Id be better at
keeping my mouth
shut.

forgive me

for still thinking you might
come back for me.

if june was a girl

she would have strawberry blonde hair that is pin straight and falls on her face just right without her even trying. she'd be the type of girl to suck on a cherry lollipop and then follow up by rubbing it across her lips, leaving a sweet red tint. she'd have butterfly clips in her hair and a small gap in her two front teeth that doesn't make her feel ugly because she knows she isn't. she is sure of herself and wears pink gingham shorts that fall just above the tips of her fingers. she drapes a white tank top over her breasts that is lined with lace and never second guesses what her twenties are for. she loves the beach and doesn't mind getting sand on the blanket she kept from her first real relationship because these things aren't worth crying over. she doesn't think about moving to different cities because her small corner of the world is just as exciting years later. she knows how to stay put and finds little things to fall in love with. she is grounded in the present moment with her loneliness and it never quite bothers her to be in her apartment alone with nothing but the sound of cicadas outside the gently cracked window. there is a porch she sits on to write poetry she is proud of in a journal she has had for too long. she loves baths and soaps and smells like a lavender-vanilla mix and she doesn't need much to stay alive for.

clean
after madisen kuhn

i wish i didn't hate that my apartment looks lived in. i wish i didn't find myself picking up after my pets and lover as though my life depends on it. it's my endless desire to feel clean that wakes me up in the morning and puts me to bed each night. it's despising the christmas lights and photos on the walls because they remind me that i do not feel at home even though i try so hard to.

i've lived in boston since 2020 and i still haven't felt like i've found my place. i still dream of the city—the one i've never been to— and swear if i could just make it there, i'd be happier. id be healthier. i'd have more of a willingness to try and get better. he tells me im crazy for this and maybe it is a little silly of me to still dream after everything i've been through but i need to. i need something to look forward to. something that will give me the courage to remind myself that i am not letting the younger me down each day i stay just out of reach of our childhood dream. the dream that looks like a corner apartment that overlooks the busy manhattan streets full of people bustling through the gloomy rainy day, and me, at my desk, writing poetry about it all.

my therapist asks me what the ideal version of me looks like and i tell her that she can handle being alone. that she actually likes being alone. the ideal version of me walks down dead streets to her favorite coffee shop and sometimes even sits inside to write. she is not scared of gaps and empty spaces or background noise. she sparks conversations with strangers and smiles at couples in central park and doesn't mind being noticed or slipping through the cracks of existence. she is who i'd be if my father wasn't so hateful and if my mother taught me self-preservation.

father's day

there is something so
pathetic about the way
i miss you sometimes.
the way you still ruin my days
and consume my nights.
not a day has gone by
where i don't think about
the little girl who just wanted
you to see her as something else.

taffy

i want to watch
different flavors
of saltwater taffy
being made in
store front windows.
i want to order
strawberry ice cream
at the general store
after a long day
of playing tag and
shitty games of
basketball.
i want to hang out
with my older cousins
and swear i'm as big
as them.
i want to beat my stepbrother
at a game of spit
and have my father put
on my water shoes
while i say i hate how
ugly they make me feel.
i want to go back to cape may
every summer
and try to bring my grandmother
back to life around
a fire pit with uncles and aunts
that say they love me
despite barely knowing me.
i want to remember what
the warm, sticky nights and
long car drives to jersey felt like.
i want to re-live the nights
on the boardwalk.

i want to spend the rest
of my life going back
to memories that felt so
fickle in the moment.
not realizing they are what
i'd keep myself alive for
as i got older.

will I ever
cradle myself
in my own bed
and not cry
for my mother

my heart has changed

is there a way
to stop time from
moving so fast.

will i ever cradle myself
in my own bed
and not cry for
my mother.

i notice the world spinning
and wonder if anyone else
can feel it too.

first loves are like the small town you grew up in

you try to forget the way it smells / the way everyone knew everyone / it hurts to think about even though it's been years / so much happened there / but there still wasn't enough time to love / first loves make infinity look so small / so you take up that space trying to grow up / or more like trying to move on / neither really happen or come to fruition / you spend your early twenties wondering when your thirties are coming / you spend your thirties wondering where the time has gone / some days you will miss your mother / other days you will understand why she hated you so much / everyday you will pull your own teeth to avoid sounding like her / your biggest regret isn't falling in love / it's falling out of it.

octaves

poetry always heals me
in the same way
that it is what i use
to abandon any sense
of taking care of myself.
instead of practicing mindfulness,
instead of sitting and accepting
the truth of the moment,
i will lay and rot into my mattress
or bathtub
and let the anger boil.
sometimes i swear i can feel
the resentment towards my
empty parents
seeping through my skin and
forming a puddle on my chest.
sometimes i am no better than
the girl who despises other girls
for being prettier
or funnier
or simpler.
less emotional and less
fuck-up.

I don't think
I can brush
my hair facing
the   mirror,

neutrality

i am worried that i'm destined
to suffer at the hands of things
out of my control
until i remember that
i am not fourteen anymore.
that i do not need to find
the perfect ending to a poem
just to make it worth
writing
or reading.
sometimes things are just there
and we have to let it be enough.
i'm not ready to be happy but
i think it's time i become more
neutral when it comes to my
emotions and existence.
i don't think i can brush my hair
facing the mirror
just yet
but i think i can stomach
it all enough
to stop putting it up in a half-assed
ponytail every day and being upset
when my scalp is sore.

space to be

i am becoming more
content with myself
as time goes on.
as i slowly get out of
this hole that i've been in—
this is what i call my early twenties.
i think the people around me
can tell
because i'm writing poetry more often
and i'm actually proud of it
for once.
i am finding myself again
and this time i'm not thirteen
and in love with older men
and hurting myself just to feel
something different.
this time i am twenty-something
and even though i think i will
always feel like a teenager,
i am the age i've always wanted
to be.
i have the autonomy i've always
dreamed of when i was a little girl
with little space to just be.

rhode island

i sat in the passenger seat
for forty five minutes and ate brunch
at a small diner i've never
heard of
in a place i've never been to.
the emptiness didn't matter
while i was sipping ginger ale
and ordering mozzarella sticks
because for a moment
i was bubbling with normalcy.

i woke up at 3am and wanted
to take a drive to shop
for cotton fabrics and sewing notions
so i did.
i felt linen blends and bought
different shades of pinks.
i wanted to be the spontaneous girl
who doesn't need to know everything
for sure,
the kind of girl who people didn't need
to worry about.
so i pushed my hair behind both ears
and made small talk with the cashier.
i laughed hard at my own jokes
on the car ride home and
played my panic off as adrenaline.
for a split second
i almost believed my own
happiness.

I almost
believed my
own happiness

enough for myself

will i ever let
being a poet
be enough?
will i ever stop wanting
to be somewhere other than
where i am?

on my own

i want to belong to someone.
i want someone to be there
when i am not strong enough
to be myself. to hold myself.
to keep myself together.
on my knees on the kitchen floor
gathering up the shards
with tears in my eyes
swearing to whatever will listen
that i am strong enough to do this
on my own
but i am so tired of picking up
my own pieces.

can a girl like me really be happy?

i'm trying to mimic
the feeling i had
yesterday
where i felt safe
and at peace
and beautiful
and full.
i filled the bath
and turned off
the light.
opened my notes app
and started writing
poetry.
i put the same song
on loop
as i try to force the feeling
of being okay.

july

it is july.
will i always be
the broken girl?
i wonder this because
i dreamt about my mother
last night
and woke up in
cold sweats
and full of ache for her.
i fell back asleep eventually
and didn't get up until
1pm.
i wasted half the day
and there is no one to blame
but myself.

what ifs

what if
everything
i love
doesn't love
me back?
what if
every time
i cry
i am asking god
to take me back?
what if
the tides never really
get smaller
and i'm left
in the sea water
forever?
what if
everything bad
that's ever happened
never really did
and i am just
good at telling stories
and not remembering
the whole truth?

too well

i can still feel
the vibrations
of left over love.
i haven't been
your girl
in a long time
yet i still wonder
who i would be
if we didn't let go.

i am drenched in desperation

i think i am meant
to be a girl in new york city
with little responsibilities
and big dreams.
a girl who doesn't wear
her hair up often
because it is always perfect
when it's down.
a girl can call her mother
and tell her about
all of the little things
and she will say
she loves me before
she hangs up.
a girl who wears her
grandmother's face—
dressed in freckles and
strawberry blonde roots.
i want a little taste
of the woman i thought
i'd be by now.
tall and bitter-less.
sweet and drenched in
something other than
desperation.

the face of a woman i've never met

i'd like to think i knew my mother.
i knew the way she yelled
when she was scared and how she
ran away from the daily sameness of
being a stay-at-home mom.
i couldn't understand it.
i still can't now—
i want the mundane things,
the familiarity of taking care of
something i love every day.
i want something in my life
to stick to me like it wants me.
my mother wanted to vanish
so she packed up her things and
somewhere in the space of our
old run-down florida home
is still a little messy-headed girl
that looks like me.

you look happier

i am white knuckling
the grudge i hold
that looks and feels like
a first love at thirteen.
i should've been able
to let go of it all by now.
forget the way it tastes
and sounds and smells.
but there is something
in every corner of every
grocery store
or hotel
or rainy day
that tells me
we still could've made it.

nightmares and night sweats

who have i become
in the midst of all
this uncertainty.
who will i be
when i wake up tomorrow
drenched in the night before.
who could i be if i stopped thinking
nothing is safe for a girl like me.

bandaids

i am writing poems
about you that i can't
stomach long enough
to finish
and all i have left to say is
where do i put
the left over vibrations
of a failed love?

great broken things

i want to write poems
that make people
care for poetry.
i want to create
and be
something beautiful.
something meaningful and
worth your while.
i don't want to be the book
you pick up and can so easily
put back down.
the one you forget about
in the bottom of your backpack
and only pull out because
you spilled water between
my pages.
i hope one day i can give myself
the meaning i'm so desperately
searching for in men and
other great broken things.
i want to find love
in poetry again.
i want to write notes
in the margins of my favorite
writer's works and never
stop talking about the one line
that changed it all.

longing for a new place to call home

there is so much
to love in the city
of boston
yet i am always finding
ways to fall out of it
and into new worlds
and hobbies
and bodies.
i cannot cup
my hands under the existence
of kind strangers and tall buildings here
and drink from it
as though it's enough.
i can only sit
in the same spot
and look out the window
pretending i'm somewhere else
for so long.

mornings and reminders

i step under the shower head
and let the warm water
wash off a scary night before.
the smell of hard boiled eggs
coming in from the crack i left
in the door
and i sway under the water
reminding myself that
i am not there anymore.

heart break hours

is it okay to still
miss my father
even though
it has been long enough
to forget him almost
entirely?

instagram poet

your poetry doesn't need
to be groundbreaking.
it just needs to move you
from one day to the next.

pixie cuts

maybe i will cut my hair
even shorter than it already is
and run away to a new city.
somewhere long and far away
from the life i have built
for myself here.
maybe then i will feel clean.
i don't know what to do
with the feeling of being unhappy
with everything i have.
maybe i am still the ungrateful girl
my father made of me.
but i know that bubble baths
and box breathing can only
help me tolerate so much
and even as i lay the covers
over my face and let
the sounds of the world outside
drown out
i am such an unhappy girl
with such a will to live
that it's making her bitter
and a little angry.

to every lover i've ever had

i will always love you
in little ways
that some days
will make me want
to rip my hair out
in giant clumps
and stare at the damage.
i will never forget
the soft days
with hard moments
in between
because i am not someone
who moves on.
i am someone
who picks up teeny tiny things
from the people she's loved
and makes them her own.

for when i need to remind myself that i am in control

i crawl into bed
so helpless
and tired.
my eyes begging to shut
for the rest of the day.
it is noon and i am done
with trying to be human.
i wish i did not let myself forget
so often
that i am not a little girl
anymore.
i can pack up my bags
and go anywhere
i want.
like to the big city or
the emergency room.
i can take care of my mind
and body and it be a good
and gentle thing.
it does not need to be an ordeal
to be alive.
it can be slow and steady
and safe.

girl best friend

i hope one day
i can dance hand in hand
in the rain
with a girl who both mirrors
and challenges me.
i want to go on adventures
around all of new england
and try different flavored
iced teas at small local places.
maybe all of this is me saying
i miss my mother
but there is so much beauty
in my desire to love and be loved.

handmade in massachusetts

lately i've been trying to make my own clothes. zig zag stitching
scrap fabric pieces onto tank tops that i want to wear all summer.
i think it's my attempt at feeling comfortable in my body. to have
more sense of control in my life.

sometimes, most of the time, my emotions take on a life of their
own. it is so hard to tell myself to stop crying. to calm down and
take a deep breath in the middle of my panic. a lot of the time it
happens when i'm alone. when i am forced to notice my cracks and
own dismemberment.

i find it grounding to make something from scratch. the way i can
sit at my sewing machine for hours on end. deep into the night.
sometimes i find myself waking up at 3am with the urge to create. to
make something worthwhile.

poetry can be like that. writing in my journal hasn't felt natural
because i haven't done it consistently since 2023. it's been two years
but im still trying to find ways back to myself. a version of me that i
have to hope isn't gone forever.

lattes and heartaches

i want to sit in a cafe
and drink matcha
with cold foam
that sticks to my upper lip.
scribbling lines in a moleskin
that i will someday turn
into something
long enough to call
poetry.
days where i finally feel like
i have the time to
stay for a while
and notice the stillness
of everything.

pretty girls

do pretty girls
panic when they
are left alone
on busy streets
surrounded by crowds
and stores closing early.
if you look at me closely
can you tell i am
only a moment away
from dropping to
the ground.
knees bent as i sit
on the curb and
watch other girls browse
vintage t-shirt racks
while they smell of victoria secret
body mist and happy endings.
will i ever know
what it feels like to
wake up refreshed and ready
for the day ahead of me
even when it is raining
and i want to succumb to
my bitter sadness.

i wonder if i will ever feel better

do you think
i will ever
stop noticing
the silence.
the empty spaces
of my apartment
that remind me
of childhood and
my mother.
is it possible to
forgive something
that has shaped you
so painfully.
will there be a day
where the sun shines
without darkening
my scars
or a night where i can
wrap myself up in
a freshly washed
thrifted quilt and doze off
without a second thought.
can i be at peace with
the things that have been
done to me in the dark
corners of my pink bedroom.
or is there always going to be
a part of me that remembers
so vividly that
i get sick to my stomach
all summer long.
drunk on violent dreams
and wondering who i could
possibly be if there was
a little less to carve out
of me.

12:02

i spent the morning
wandering through
thrift stores looking for
a hidden treasure.
something that might
make me feel better in
the peak of my nightmares.
it is summer and the windows
are finally open again
but i feel the same as i did
when it was below freezing.
all want, all yearn, all pine
and no living the life
i've always wanted.
no getting out of bed and
cleaning my apartment by
lighting candles and vacuuming
up cat litter.
i remember the snow being so
beautiful in the busy parts
of boston
but i forgot that winter
can stretch across my
entire being and make me
close my eyes and lock them shut
by gluing my palms to my face
long enough to miss the moments
when things feel easy.

cherry street

i used to sneak out of
the front gate of my mothers house
on cherry street
in a small town in florida
when i was fourteen.
i would walk to the park
a couple blocks away
and sit in the mist of the
half-shitty weather.
i'd sit on a bench
and wonder if i'd ever
outgrow the small space
of my bedroom.
if life would ever get easier
or more worth it.
sometimes i'd wander the
surrounding woods
with my older brother
and the adventures had us
running through strangers
backyards
hoping we don't get caught.
i think we were both a little sick.
sick of wanting things we
couldn't seem to have.
i think we were all we had
and for the longest time
that kept me alive.
now that it's been years
down the line
and i don't know what
they're up to, or where they live
or who they love,
i try to let the memories
soften me.

rooted

i wish i could stay somewhere
long enough to put down roots.
i want the coffee shop down
the street to know my order
by heart.
to greet me as a friend
when i come in to write
in my journal until closing.
i wish life felt as beautiful
as i want to feel.
i want to sit by the pool
for longer than an hour
and not mind burning
under the sun.

maybe i will feel better when i am older

i spend sunny days wishing
things were different.
i spend warm and fuzzy months
begging myself to get better.
it feels like all i can do is
tell myself i will
feel better when
i am older.
when i am wise
and know more
than i do right now.
though i am scared
i will always be somewhat
clueless as to what
the whole point of
everything is.

the sun is shining and i am alive

it's the perfect weather today.
it's friday and i feel as free
as i possibly can as someone
who is scared of everything.
i'm eating at a local pizza place
with my lover and i don't fall apart
over the fact that my freckles are
more noticeable in the sun.
i'm writing stupid poetry
on my phone
and somehow
for the first time in so long
it feels like enough.
i feel like enough.

too young

my mouth is full
of cheese pizza
in cambridge massachusetts
and i look out the window
in front of me
and see an older woman
who looks a lot like
my grandma did.
even her hair is cut
the same way.
that same shade
of auburn with choppy ends.
it reminds me to live a little.
to put down the knife and
stop twisting it in
my own back.

thoughts on growing up

i like listening to covers by cavetown and taking baths full of lavender essential oils. i light a candle and shut the door and let the warm steam fill my lungs and clear my nose. how beautiful is it that i can spend all day writing poetry even if no one reads it?

i have learned to love my writing over the past few days. i'm cutting myself a break and being proud of the things i do. it's taken so much time to feel even an ounce of happiness when it comes to what i write and how i write it. now that i feel it, i want to revel in it. i'm craving the sensation in my chest that joy brings me. it's not just about being happy, it's about being grounded and in the moment. i didn't know what that meant for the longest time but as the acceptance comes, so does the will to live.

even though i hate the length my hair is at and i want to cut it all off, i'm still trying to grow it out. i'm sitting with the discomfort of feeling ugly and unlovable. i'm dealing with this dislike i have towards myself. everyday i'm becoming less and less hard on myself. tolerance is key in adulthood. it's something i've had to teach myself. i didn't grow up with picture perfect—or even close to that—demonstrations of how to take care of oneself.

growing up for me meant making a lot of mistakes and not only hurting the people i love but hurting myself. the choices i made when i was a teenager still follow me as i enter my first big quarter-life-crisis. my point is, despite the lack of lessons my parents taught me that were beneficial, i'm still here. i'm still doing what i can to stay alive and stay at peace. because that's all i really want. to feel a sense of peace and contentment when i look at the spaces around me. i want to let the chaos of childhood sit in a box in my closet that i only open when i'm feeling nostalgic and miss my brother. not when i'm looking for a way out of my beautiful and simple and complicated life.

am i doing this right?

i'm trying to mimic
the feeling i had
yesterday
where i felt safe
and at peace
and beautiful
and full.
i filled the bath
and turned off
the light.
opened my notes app
and started writing
poetry.
i put the same song
on loop
as i try to force the feeling
of being okay.

tide

the world moves.
it spins and with each season,
the earth dies
and breathes
again. it teaches me this lesson
of saving yourself even when
there is so little life left.

the ocean
never stops crashing into
the shore.
even when the sun
is gone and there is no one to see it
prove it's humanity.
i am so scared of
falling off deep ends and
not being able to do more
than just graze the bottom
with the tip of my toes
and i wonder if i'm getting
in the way of
the current
each time i cry and admit that i miss
thinking i can change the past.

confessions of a quarter-life-crisis

if i've learned anything about being a daughter—the eldest one— it's that you're going to be so many people yet still feel like you're never getting better. never changing. i'm almost halfway to thirty and all i can do is hope that i will be in a different place by the time i become the age i swear my mother still is.

i want to live in the city. i don't know if or when i will move from the home i have in boston, but i know that each day i am here, i am letting the smaller version of me down.

i can't remember the last time i heard my own laugh and didn't recognize my brother within it. as an eldest daughter i've also learned that it's so hard to be your own person. to form a self outside of what you've been through. this is especially true for the fragmented girls. the ones with so many wholes that they form a collective, or several.

i sit in bed with aching limbs from moving the furniture throughout my apartment and my throat burns from swearing i will leave it this way forever. i am always moving. always looking for somewhere to put the skin i've shed.

i don't remember my mother's voice, and i've done my best to forget the way my father's face is shaped. but it's all with me. it's the bipolar rage. the borderline suspicions. i am still the red-headed girl with the french braided hair curling up on the couch after swimming in the deep end for too long. it's soggy skin and hot dogs wrapped in cheese slices. its the end of the world and there is nothing left.

i've loved all the wrong things. all the wrong boys and men. it was so easy to fall victim again and again. even after i swore i never would again. i've been a ghost longer than i've been a girl and the thing about dying is it never really happens to you. i cry at the notebook and thirteen going on thirty and it's in those moments that i am most myself but i will never not be ashamed to admit it.

i am in a hole at my young yet i-feel-old-age and there is nothing left for me but wishing i had my mother to guide me through the heartbreaks i put myself through. it's always the right person, wrong time, yet they don't tell you how to recover from a man who can get away with evil.

a burning sensation

i write about
being a girl
because that's where
the pain is.
that's where
the fire starts.

in this world

today i will move through
the weeds of remembering
and try not to let myself
suffer at the hands of childhood.
i will be big, and grown up.
i will clean my apartment and
make breakfast
as though it is
any other warm june day.
the night before, the one with
the cold sweats and visitations,
will slip off my body as though it's
just another sweater in the transitional
summer months of every year.
i will forget what i dreamt about
and it won't matter much at all.
the kicking and the screaming
is only metaphorical in this world.
the world where i am not steeped
in the toxic coating of growing up
a girl.

maybe my father was right

i am something worth leaving
when i am so upset that i gnaw at
chunks of my hair while its still attached
to my scalp.
when i am crying so hard
that i am convinced there is no air left
on earth for someone like me.
someone who is too soft
for her own good
and others.
someone who will spend the rest
of her life looking for someone
who will love her despite the many
lazy days and broken home she
comes from.

suddenly

vienna by billy joel plays on repeat on the second of april. a day where the sun is shining but the air is crisp and sharp around the edges. suddenly i am twenty three and need to disappear. suddenly i am twelve again and have been invisible my whole life. it all floods back to me and now i am sinking into a porcelain bathtub wishing i could be more brave.

self-destruction

i don't know what to do
when it comes to my indifference
towards you.
most days
i can't believe
i knew you.
that i loved you and wanted
to keep loving you.

words i'm still holding onto

you tell me you love me
and i tell you that you couldn't
like me any less.
you look me up and down
and i look you in the eyes.
i'm so far from who you thought
you'd love at this age.

i wanted to sink my teeth into something real

because i'm convinced that i'm not.
there are so many times a day
where my skin is numb
and my hands are both heavy
and nothing.

i'm not doing well

in another world
i am a girl who does not
think about her first love
or the gaps of her father.
i am in the moment and fearless.
i can eat men for breakfast
and i am not afraid of myself
in a silent room.

breakthrough

i tell myself
that i don't need anyone
when i am bawling my eyes out
on a bathroom floor
covered in nothing but
my own shame.
i am always so certain that
i can do this on my own.
i am so determined to prove
my strength to anyone
who will look in my direction.
this is my way of saying
i am so angry that i might always
live out of spite.

shame is a story i tell myself

the room falls dark
and all i am is
a vessel within it.
i can only replay the positives
so many times
before it sounds like
a lie i tell myself
to keep me going.

ritualistic

i exist in
silhouettes
and bedroom
closets
with palms over
my eyes.
i am scared of
big guys and
nighttime.
am i brave
enough
to sleep in
my own bed
and close
my eyes
every night.
when i inevitably
wake up
scared of
the past
will i be able
to remember that
it's been long
gone.

the next big great thing

am i nothing in
this big world
full of greatness and
endless possibilities.
is taking a bath
and following my dreams
full of poetry
important enough,
worth it enough,
to keep doing it.
i wonder what i will do
right before i die.
if my life will flash
and my heart will pang
with regret and fear.
or if i will know
that i kept myself alive
despite it all
and lived everyday
as though it was worth it,
as though i was.

slowing down because i'm safe now

how do i slow down.
take in the scent of
the day after
it downpours.
the smell of wet cement
and fall candles in
the peak of summer.
will i remember my life
as something beautiful.
will i clench my fist at
my father forever.
when will i learn to
let go and relax
the muscles in
my face.
the tension in my shoulders
and the fear down
my spine.
all of it keeping me
from seeing the beauty
in what is here
and what no longer is.

the girl who fell through the cracks

living for myself
has never come
easy to me.
i have learned how
to take care of
every little living thing.
everything but myself.

Afterword

i hope you don't think of me differently after reading through the things i have lived and felt and thought throughout my life. i've spent the last year working on this book and just hoping and maybe even praying, that it doesn't sound too repetitive.

it's true that everyday has felt the same for me over the past year. i've gotten stuck and unstuck over and over again this year and part of it was me worrying that this project would never fully be what i wanted it to be; something worth reading. i'm tired of writing things that i'm not proud of. things that couldn't matter any less. i've also dug myself in and out of holes all year. wondering who i am when i'm sad and angry. if i look anything like my mother when i sigh too many times in a day.

i've tried to be proud of myself for the little things. things like still being able to feel after all i've been through. though sensitivity is not always something i feel i'm gifted with. more of than not, the existence of my emotions and their intensity feels like a curse passed onto me by my mother. and the worst part is, i don't have her to tell me it's okay to cry.

this book is my way of saying i'm sorry to myself for not letting myself be happier even when i was begging for it.

You can find Gracie Drew on instagram @poetgracie.